Please return or renew this item by the last date shown.
You may renew items (unless they have been requested
by another customer) by telephoning, writing to or calling
in at any library. ♻ 100% recycled paper   *BKS 1 (5/95)*

Wild Britain

Hills and Mountains

Louise and Richard Spilsbury

www.heinemann.co.uk
Visit our website to find out more information about Heinemann Library books.

To order:
☎ Phone 44 (0) 1865 888066
🗎 Send a fax to 44 (0) 1865 314091
🖥 Visit the Heinemann Bookshop at www.heinemann.co.uk to browse our catalogue and order online.

First published in Great Britain by Heinemann Library, Halley Court, Jordan Hill, Oxford OX2 8EJ, part of Harcourt Education Ltd. Heinemann is a registered trademark of Harcourt Education Ltd.

Editorial: Lucy Thunder and Helen Cox
Design: David Poole and Celia Floyd
Illustrations: Alan Fraser and Geoff Ward
Picture Research: Catherine Bevan and Peter Morris
Production: Sevy Ribierre

Originated by Dot Gradations
Printed and bound in Hong Kong, China by South China Printing

ISBN 0 431 03918 6
07 06 05 04 03
10 9 8 7 6 5 4 3 2 1

British Library Cataloguing in Publication Data
Spilsbury, Louise and Spilsbury, Richard
Hills and mountains. – (Wild Britain)
577.5'3'0941
A full catalogue record for this book is available from the British Library.

Acknowledgements

The Publishers would like to thank the following for permission to reproduce photographs: Bruce Colemann pp4 (Martin Guppy), 13, 27 (Robert Maier), 21 (Allan G Potts), 23 (Tom Schandy); Corbis pp5, 6 (Annie Griffiths Belt), 7 (John Heseltine), 8 (Ecoscene), 12 (Andrew Brown/Ecoscene), 14 (Steve Austin), 15, 28; FLPA pp11 (M J Thomas), 16 (Robert Canis), 17 (M Clark), 18 (Brian Turner) 19 (Tony Hamblin), 20, 25, 26 (M Callan) 22 (Foto Natura Stock); GSF Picture Library pp9, 29; Photodisc p24; Rex Features p10.

Cover photograph of Derwentwater from the slopes of the Catbells, Brandelhow Estate, Cumbria, reproduced with permission of National Trust Photographic Library (Joe Cornish).

The publishers would like to thank Michael Scott for his assistance in the preparation of this book.

Every effort has been made to contact copyright holders of any material reproduced in this book. Any omissions will be rectified in subsequent printings if notice is given to the Publisher.

Contents

What are hills and mountains? 4

Hill and mountain habitats 6

Changes 8

Living there 10

Moorland plants 12

Plants higher up 14

Insects 16

Adders and lizards 18

Mountain birds 20

Birds of prey 22

Mountain hares 24

Red deer 26

Dangers 28

Food chain 30

Glossary 31

Index 32

Any words appearing in the text in bold, **like this**, are explained in the Glossary.

What are hills and mountains?

Mountains, like these in Scotland, are much higher than hills.

Hills and mountains are pieces of land that are higher than the ground around them. A mountain is just a very big hill.

A hill or mountain habitat like this provides living things with food, water and **shelter**.

A **habitat** is the natural home of a group of plants and animals. In this book we look at some plants and animals that live, grow and **reproduce** in hill and mountain habitats.

Hill and mountain habitats

This is the moorland level of a mountain. Moorland is covered in short plants, grasses, heather and a few trees.

At the bottom of a tall hill or mountain it is warm enough for many trees and plants to grow. Higher up, it is colder, wetter and windier. Here, the land becomes **moorland**.

At the top of this mountain, green moss and yellow lichen grow on the rocks.

High up a mountain it is too cold for many plants to grow. Only small plants grow here. They grow low so they stay out of the path of the wind.

Changes

This hill gets the full heat of the Sun in summer. There are few trees to shade the land from the Sun.

Weather can change quickly on high hills and mountains. In summer, it can be very hot during the day. Then it becomes very cold at night.

In winter, rain often collects in bogs like this. The ground and plants have soaked up water like a sponge.

In autumn and winter, it can be icy cold on hills and mountains. Storms and winds blow across the land. Many mountain birds **migrate** to warmer places.

Living there

Only a few small **insects**, spiders and worms live at the top of a mountain. This is an earwig.

Few animals live at the top of high hills or mountains. It is too cold, and there are no big plants to **shelter** under and feed on.

Farmers often leave their cows, goats, sheep and ponies on the lower levels of a hill or mountain.

More animals live on the **moorland** level. These include deer, foxes, rabbits and mice. Birds fly over all levels of a mountain but mainly hunt over moorland. There are more animals there for them to catch.

Moorland plants

The mountain ash has flowers in spring and bright red berries in autumn. Many different birds eat these fruits.

Cold winds sweep across **moorland** and the **soil** is shallow. Most plants are short, such as grasses and heathers. The mountain ash that grows here is a short tree.

Bilberries are the fruits of the bilberry plant. Many birds and animals eat these berries.

Many mountain animals, including rabbits and deer, eat leaves or berries. Gorse and other mountain plants have spikes or thorns. These stop some animals from eating them.

Plants higher up

Moss campion plants grow close together, near the ground.
They look like colourful cushions.

Many high mountain plants grow close to
the ground. This keeps them out of the wind
and the cold. Some, such as blue gentian and
pink moss campion, have colourful flowers.

These colourful pink flowers are called primulas. They grow in the cracks of rock on hills and mountains.

Some mountain plants grow in cracks among the rocks. The rocks give them **shelter** from the wind and cold. Frost and strong winds can harm plant parts.

Insects

This is a crane fly. **Female** crane flies lay eggs underground. The young eat underground plant parts.

Many flies, grasshoppers and beetles live in mountains in summer. Most of these **insects** only live for a short time. They lay eggs underground before they die. The eggs **hatch** out the following spring.

This mountain butterfly, called a grayling, is feeding on heather.

Some mountain insects, such as midges and horse flies, feed on animal blood. Others, like bees and butterflies, feed on **nectar** from the centre of flowers.

Adders and lizards

An adder uses venom (poison) to catch animals to eat. The poison comes out of its long front teeth when it bites.

An adder is a snake with a zig-zag pattern on its back. Adders live underground on **moorland** or hills. They eat small animals such as voles, snails and lizards.

On hills and mountains common lizards, like this, lie on rocks to soak up the Sun.

Snakes and lizards are **reptiles**. Common lizards are brown with dark side stripes and white flashes. They catch and eat spiders and **insects**.

Mountain birds

Curlews spend spring and summer on open **moorland**. They often make their nests on the ground.

Many birds, such as golden plovers, stonechats and wheatears visit mountains. They come in spring to have their young. Many make their **nests** in the short grass.

Red grouse can live on mountains all year round because their food – heather – grows there all year.

Many birds **migrate** for the winter. Some birds, like grouse, live on mountains all year round. Adult grouse eat the green **shoots** of heather plants.

Birds of prey

Buzzards fly high over mountains. They have excellent eyesight so they can spot small animals on the ground.

Birds of prey fly over mountains and hills. They swoop down and catch small animals to eat. Owls, ravens and buzzards eat **reptiles**, mice and birds.

Golden eagles fly high looking for animals to eat. They then swoop down to catch them.

Golden eagles are huge birds of prey. Their wings, from tip to tip, measure about 2 metres. They eat rabbits, foxes, hares and grouse.

Mountain hares

Mountain hares often come out at night to eat heather and grass.

In the daytime, mountain hares rest in scrapes. Scrapes are dips in the ground that they dig with their paws. Some hares live in holes in the ground called burrows.

A mountain hare's white winter hair helps it to hide in the snow.

Foxes, stoats and **birds of prey** feed on mountain hares. In summer, mountain hares have grey hair to **camouflage** them against rocks. In winter, their hair turns white to hide them in snow.

Red deer

Red deer are the biggest mountain animals in Britain.

In summer, red deer live high up in mountains. They eat grasses and **shoots**. In winter, they move to lower ground to eat heather and bilberry plants.

In autumn, red deer gather to have young.

Male red deer are called stags. Each year the antlers (horns) on their head fall off and new ones grow. **Female** deer are called hinds. They do not have antlers.

Dangers

If a moorland fire gets out of control, it burns too many plants. Bare soil may then be damaged by the wind.

People burn **moorland** heather sometimes. This helps to keep the heather healthy. It is bad if the fire gets too strong because it then kills other plants and seeds.

This mountain path in Wales has been used too much. The rocks and soil have been worn away.

Lots of people walk and climb on hills and mountains. It is important that they keep to footpaths. If they walk elsewhere they can wear away pieces of the land.

Food chain

All plants and animals in a hill or mountain **habitat** are connected through the food they eat. Food chains show how different living things are linked. Here is one example:

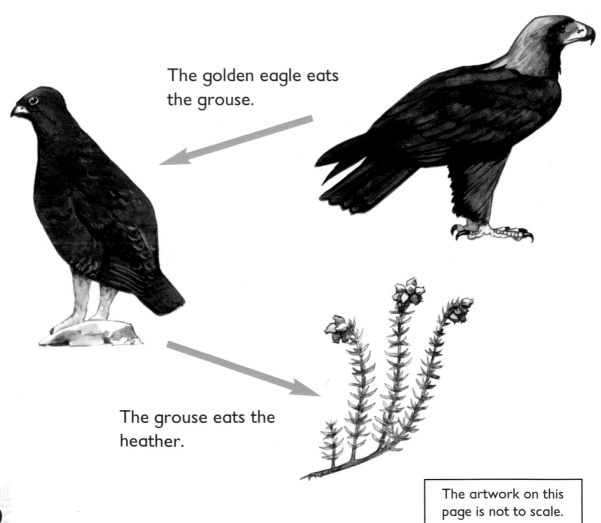

The golden eagle eats the grouse.

The grouse eats the heather.

The artwork on this page is not to scale.

Glossary

birds of prey birds that hunt and catch animals to eat

camouflage when animals have colours or patterns that make them hard to see

female female animals can lay eggs or give birth to live young

habitat the natural home of a group of plants and animals

hatch to be born from an egg

insects small animal that has six legs when an adult

male animal which can become a father when it is grown up. A male human is a man or a boy.

migrate when animals move to a warmer place for the winter

moorland cool windy area covered by heather and other shrubs, usually quite high up a hill or mountain

nectar sweet, sugary juice in the centre of a flower, which insects eat

nest something an animal makes to rest or to have young in

reproduce when plants and animals make young just like themselves

reptile animals with scales, such as lizards and snakes

shelter somewhere safe to stay, live or have young

shoots young stem, leaves and flowers of a plant

soil also called mud or earth. Soil is made up of lots of different things, including tiny bits of rock and dead plants.

Index

animals 5, 10, 11, 13, 18, 22, 23, 26, 30

autumn 9, 27

birds 9, 11, 12, 13, 20–21, 22–23, 25

bogs 9

flowers 14, 15, 17

heather 6, 12, 21, 24, 26, 28

insects 10, 16, 17, 19

moorland 6, 11, 12, 18, 20, 28

plants 5, 6, 7, 9, 10, 12, 13, 14–15, 16, 21,
   26, 28, 30

reptiles 19, 22

spring 16, 20

summer 8, 16, 20, 25, 26

trees 6, 8, 12

weather 6, 8–9

winter 9, 21, 25, 26